deeper,
still

deeper,
still

Brittany Bronte

44 Suns Publishing

The Stranger in my Car

So even though
You ran your fingers up my spine
And collected my hair in a way
So I had no choice
But to part my lips
And to part my legs
Unlocking that slit
Of a space
You claimed
As yours
You left me on read
And the words unsaid
Between us
Evaporated into the air

The Offer

I'll be your safe place
The space to lay your head
And to trace with your hands
My heart
Is big, soft, and open
A perfect Pillow
And a token reminder
Of all I have
To offer you

The Parking Lot

When my legs shook
And I couldn't stand
Lust spilling out
And down my thighs
And you whispered,
Don't worry, I got you
And I gripped the back of your neck
And let go

Colors

I hear you in a song
And the memory reaches in
And squeezes me tight
While I hold my breath
And hold up the colors
The ones behind my eyes
Into the light

Peter Pan

Like a lost boy
In the trees
You please only yourself
Under palms with your beads
And teased hair
Unaware of the lives you wreck
Or don't you even care?
You stand all proud
And golden
With your grand ego
Flicked across the sand
With your cigarette
And you're set
And I regret ever meeting you
A lost boy in the trees
And I, your Wendy

Last Call

I'm the sun on your shoulders
In the morning dawn
I'm the uber when the bartender
Says you're done
I take every inch of you
And make it my own
Every inch
Slick and wet
And bring it home

Hope

There's something inside
Between the cages
Where ages of days are dry as bone
Like a bird with fluttering wings
it tickles and reminds
Me of that feeling....
What's that feeling?
The one that spreads light
Across mountainscapes
And chases from the corners
All the shadows away
There's something inside
It feels like I'm not alone
To throw stones
At myself in the morning
Like a warm hug
It tugs at my arms
And throws away time
And reminds
Me of that feeling...
What's that feeling?
The one that creeps up legs
And gives strength to jump
And fills empty arms
With promises of something

The Slip

You step out of my love
As easily
As I slip out of my silk robe
Falling in shiny folds on the floor
Are all the words ignored
They gather around my feet
With their jagged edges
Leaving me with worry
About where next I thread

Wish

I wish I never knew
There could be a love
Like you
Even though
I truly don't know
If it was real or a feeling
I was desperate to believe in
My life is on its head
Trying to make sense
Of where to send
My dreams to rest
So I wish I never knew
There could be a love
Like you

The Bath

You reach in
And pull the plug
My secrets spilling out
Running down my legs
And soaking my shoes
And you do it again
For good measure
And leave me standing
In a puddle spent

The Good Dishes

Sailing the seas
Between reefs of jagged
Edges and smooth shores
Never before
Have I seen this place
Faced with the choice
Of this or that
I tapped out
Of a life well-lived
And justly deserve
To be served on the good dishes
All my wishes
The ones deep seeded
And retreated
And all I had to do was be aware
Part my lips
And out they spilled
Like birds from a cage

The Necklace

I hate your blue eyes and sly smile
The kind that shines
And holds a secret
I hate your strong neck that held the beads
That would hang down
And fall in my face
When we made love
I hate your long legs
And the way the muscle would clench in your thighs
When I feasted
It's a beast
This thing
And now your face
Hides behind a haze in my mind
And I can't wait
Until it leaves me

Killing Time

Be my distraction
A pretty place to hang my hat
While the days drag on and on
Be my kill-time
My extra five and dime
Because I know what it feels like
To be offered the world
In a single cup of coffee
Because I know
What it feels like
To see yourself
Your future
And your past
In a single smile
Be my distraction...
For just a little while

The Giver

So much love I had
It wrapped around you 10,000-fold
And bounced between your ears
And like a mirror in the sunlight
It reflected back
And blinded me....so it was enough
To light the way
For both of us

The Hibiscus

Ripe and ready
Radiant in the sun
Pistil quivers in the wind
And reaches out
A loaded gun

Hermes

Gorgeous curves and hard edges
The juxtaposition
Of being rugged and being beautiful
He glides across the water
Like Hermes
Chiseled and quick footed
He could glide for miles
And behind him he looks
And smiles
But not too wide
Equally embarrassed
And equally flattered
And I think it's a sad wonder
We do not know the beauty and the strength
In the lines of our own backs

The Match

Is it enough yet?
Have I made you hate me?
Just like the dance of the sun and the moon
We will never dance together...
And just like the Earth
After a harvest of 7 years
It's time to scorch the fields
And burn it all to the ground
So is it enough yet?
Have I made you hate me?
Because if you can't love me...
I need you to

The Swimmer

He told me once
About a swimmer
How they can move
Through the water like a fish
Using the body
To cut through currents
Or riding with them
How simply splitting your fingers
Would have the water
Bending to your will
And with his sun kissed skin
And dark eyes
Of a writer- unrealized
I took his lips in mine
And we dove into passion
Like diving into the sea

Religion

You want me to wash you
Of all your sins
And to make you
Some more
The kind of sins
That feel like religion
And the tension
between your legs
Is aching for me
To be your whore

The Dish

Open hips
In two hands
Sweet nectar
Overflows
Dining
On my lips
Dying
And being
Reborn
All at once

The Need

The Painful ecstasy
Of disrobing souls
And diving in
Seeking shelter in skin

Bedrooms

You keep me in a palace
Of white clouds and pillows
Trading dreams
And signing our name
To each one
With careful calligraphy
And for every letter
Holding my breath

The Storm

Your breath is
Mountain air
And rainstorms
Melting into you this night
I evaporate
And feel utterly safe
And utterly shattered
At the same time

Gently

Go gentle into the day
When the memories fade away
And light pours onto your mistakes
When the glare of it all
Is too much to take
Go gentle into the day

The Moon in June

Summer moon
Of a bold and quiet June
Walking with the pace
Of future places to be
And comparisons between
Her and me
Summer moon
Of gone too soon
Time stealing away
The last hours of night
And us playing and staying
Until the first sight of light

Twilight

2 feet on the ceiling
And then 2 more...
Like an invitation
To open the floor
Like a bidding
To open the flood gates...
A time for spilling secrets
For each other's sake
And we worry about the mess tomorrow
After the sunrise of another day

Meadow Song

Take me to the spot
Where we can be free
The spot that waits
For just you and me
Where the birds hold their breath
To make room for our song
And the reeds dance in the wind
To sing along

Sweet Wine

I'm spoiled
And I'm ruined
I've had the sweetest grapes…
Tastes of the sweetest wine
It withstands time
And notions
A love potion-notwithstanding
At the end of his stem
A full-bellied love requiem
No other grape
Not red, black, or green
Could satisfy me
Just his
The sweetest taste
I'm ruined
And I'm spoiled
And desperately thirsty

Flight Music

I feel your heartbeat
In the cadence of our song
A memory that reaches
Inside dark creases
To shed light
On the possibility
Of tomorrow

Cannibal

Collecting bones...
The last fragments
Of connecting parts
To pick my teeth on
And suck dry

Scabs

There are no more words
Left to say
They've been poured out
Every last one
Dried and crusty
On the edge of the table
And breaking nails
To scrape them off

Fake Plastic Parts

Between sheets
And over miles
Piles of plastic pieces
Filling up my mind
Covering up the time
Like a past life...
When you loved me

Trades

A walking melancholy tune
Radiohead in bloom
You are
Blowing excuses
From the ends of your smoke
And that's what draws me in
Our satire lives of a joke-
Like a flippant remark
We trade demons
In the dark

West Coast Baby

West coast baby
With a New York style
Run your hands across me
I'm your Emerald Isle
Tangled legs in bed
"Let's stay here awhile"
Lost in your lust
And dying
With a smile

A Story Awaits

I lay out for you
Naked and bare
Like a clean paper piece
Pen on me
What your heart desires
And that's what I'll be

Pound for Pound

Clenching my legs
Around his waist
Like a lock and chain
He's pounding out
What's left of you
Driving your name
Further away
From my mind
With each drain

2 Lovers

Tangled legs
And arms that begin
And end like a river
And that sliver of hope
To forget all that they know
Over white folds
And hidden
Underneath
Are 2 lovers
Beneath

Writer's Embrace

Hemingway and Wilde
In dusty jackets
Looking down from the shelf
At a lover's embrace
And their struggle
To have a poet's mind
And an artist's eyes
In a world without grace

Morning Gifts

You give me
Sunrises
And honeyed words
That baptize me
Washing clean
The faded
And ragged dreams
Of yesterday
And leave me sticky
With wanting more

The Bohemian

You're a beautiful mess
With your cynical west
Coast smile
Traveling miles
With piles
Of bags stacked high
Invisible denial
Of all that
You are running from

I Would/ You Would

If I could
Swallow you up
Every last inch
Or take you in
Like a warm sheath
So deep inside me
You'd forget her name

Come

I wouldn't go
Unless you went with me
But you went
Without me
And I took you in
And kept every last drop
Wishing only
To have held your gaze
Until you collapsed
In a hazy daze

Sugar

Pouring my heart out
Like a sweet tea on a summer's day
And the residue is sticky
On your lips
Just the same

The Embrace

Thirsty we were
And drunk we became

Empty Spaces

Across gulfs of a divide
We reside and agree
To meet in the middle
Grazing the remnants of shadows
And just out of reach
It never seems quite real
Just a feeling
Of left-over wishes
And hoping to extinguish
The cobwebs

A Christmas Carol

When I leaned in and saw
In equal parts
Fear and yearning
Behind your eyes
Like the red shine of my lips
Was going to reach in
And rip your heart out
To leave you to die
But you couldn't resist anyway
But to try

Passion

Your breath covers me
Warming my shoulders
Flowing down my breasts
And wraps us
In a cloudy cocoon

Breathing

In the crook
Of your neck
And in the warmth
Above your thighs
That soft skin
Behind your ear
And on the summit
Of your shoulder's rear
That hollow place
In the center of your chest
Where my chin
Can rest...
Is the best
Of my memories
And where my soul goes
To breath

Branded

You lit a fire in me
That I'll forever chase
With reckless abandon
And screaming are the days
Of urgency
Like I've been forever branded

The Great Escape

Grab on
And we'll fly up
And over their heads
To where the field awaits
And the flowers, a bed
Made just for us
And where the rain
Tastes like freedom

How many?

How many miles
Will it take
To forget the days
We had
Because I would walk
Over 10,000 miles
To erase the curve
Of your face
From my mind

10,000 Years

Just a word
A single word
And I'd swim
To the ends of the earth
And wait 10,000 years
For a day
A single day
To kiss you up
And show you the treasures
Of all your worth

Birthday Poem

Once a child of the road
Now a man of the sea
Set free
By the words of Kerouac
Collecting people
And harvesting stories
And the glory
Of experiences
From the west coast to the east
Once a child of the road
Now a man of the sea

Giving

I give all of myself
And I offer it gladly
If I get hurt
It's only because
You will choose
How you will use
What I give you
If I get hurt
It's only because
I gave all of myself
And I offered it gladly
The love inside me
Is in abundance
And I will make more
And it will cover my wounds
And my skin will grow
Even stronger
Then before

Heaven

You think of me
Your walking wet dream
With my shiny lips
And Heaven
In my open hips

Please

He said,
"I wish there was something
I could do for you."
And she thought...
There is.
Split yourself open
And pour out the mess-
That beautiful mess
So I can dig around
And find the parts
That look like mine

The Collection

Looking for pieces of you
In everyone I meet
A laugh and a smile
The way you walk when you're excited
And the way you sigh
When your contented
So one day
My collection of parts
Might equal a minute
I can spend with you

Oh Despair

Oh despair
I'll nurture and keep you there
In my chest
With a lock and key
I'll take you everywhere
The best of friends
You are to me
Oh Despair
I'll never let you go
I'll water you and you'll grow
Spreading seeds
Of memories
Sprinkling over me
Oh despair
Even in the dark
With your remarkable
Sadness
I'll smile through the tears
Erasing wasted years
Because oh despair
You're the only place
I can still find him
Is there

Ophelia

And the lady
In her beauty
And fist full of posies
Submerges into the cold
Her hair swirling and shining
Like fire underwater
And the lilies
And the fish
Welcome her home
Where she is forever unrequited

The Suffered

The most tragic part
Isn't that we can't be together
Or that you don't love me anymore
The tragedy
Is that your beautiful smile
And the light behind your eyes
Are gone
And the exponential love
That overflowed from us
And poured into everyone else
Has dried up
And we are lonely sufferers
Not suffering alone

Black Hole

That fantastic pull
Keeping us in orbit
Circling each other
Closer and closer
Until the beautiful crash
And all the collateral damage
Scattered about
That was left
Changes worlds
As we spin off
In opposite directions
Each to our own universe

The Sagittarius

With your slim
And trim stance
And a glance
That could sizzle trees
You move
Through cities
And worlds
With your arrow and bow
And you think you know
That your magic is greatest alone
But darling with mine
It'll light the world on fire
And our desires will reign
Around the globe

Energy

Even thousands of miles away
You pull the light from me
Those shining eyes
In disguise
And avoiding
All the toiling
You pull the light from me
And I let you
Dancing in dreams
It seems
Is all we have
And the light
Oh that light that shines
In my bones and leaves me
Feeling electric

The Sweetest Fruit

I seep through
The crevices of your mine
You try and hide
But my smells
And the swells
Of your pants
Keep us in this cosmic dance
I'm a healer
And a dealer of dreams
And you can't resist
But to pluck me from the tree
Take a bite and whisper all your secrets
Swallow me down
And breathe me in
Count to 10
The whirlwind is about to begin

Redemption

Over mountains
And over hills
The thrill of the tongue
The one that whispers
And spreads
Hot breath
Between my legs
Over roads
And in caves
Craving you to ooze
Into the crevices
Finding redemption
And death
At the same time

To Begin Again

You gave me your heart
But I needed your soul
And to go
And grow into a woman
With hands to hold
The slippery edges
Of your mold
You gave me your soul
And I give you mine
You needed the time
To find
The grip
To hold the slips
And loose ends
And now
Here's to second beginnings

Wanted

You cannot fuck my body
If you don't want to fuck my soul
And it knows
Who wants to follow
The road
To tales and stories
Untold
It knows
Who wants to make love
To its secrets
In dark places
And there is no room
For spaces
In between

One

Curves
Smooth
Squeezing
Teasing
Pushing
Pulling
Wet
Slippery
Hot
Lost
In
Ecstasy

The Rider

Taking courage
By the reins
I lay you down
And mount you
Like a stallion
Riding hard and fast
To cover miles
Of loneliness
In my past

The Risk

Senses exploding
Regret foreboding
Reckless abandon
For you will be holding
Me down
And pounding away
The last pieces of indecision

Hooded Eyes

I can't put my finger on it
That time we were riding away
The miles of passed time
And the look in your eyes
Like half of them were blind
And the other half…
I can't put my finger
Was the destination
To pain or to pleasure?
Riding away the miles
As the hours were flying by
Without ever leaving the parking lot

Morning Sex

The early morning sun rises
And you enter
Moving together
We welcome the day
Quivers move from belly to toes
As if the sun knows
And blesses us
And all that's left to say

The Last Drop

Wanting all of you
The dark shadows behind your eyes
The ease of your smile
The length of your thigh
Every drop of juice
Inside of you
I want it all to be mine
I'll take nothing less
The words you hold back
The empty caresses
I want more
All the overgrown paths
Behind the bends of your soul
I'll take nothing less
But all of you

Let's Dance

Lay me down
Like a flower
Crumbling
Each Petal
Smooth between your fingers
And open
Breaking into pieces
In your arms

A Silk Robe

I just want to be...
Perpetually drenched
And deliciously sticky
With sore legs
With bruises on my thighs
Walking around to greet the day
A coffee cup
An opened robe
And a soft breeze
Cooling down the skin
That's holding onto fire

The Scent of Sex

The smell of
Desire
Mountain sides
And green shires
Rain-soaked skin
And the hot smells
Of beginning again
The smell of
Spice
And whispers of long past nights
On the streets of New York
Brownstone steps
And the sweetness of sweat
The smell of
Passion
And moonlit nights
The smell of the sea
And neon bar lights
Twinkling bright
Like the fire in your eyes

What a Girl Wants

Don't tell me I'm hot
I know I ooze sex
With every breath I take
Tell me I'm beautiful
That my smile shines light
On the darkest of days
and my eyes has the only pool
you wish to drown
Tell me I'm an adventure
That you want to get lost
In the nooks and crannies
Behind my rib cage
And never be found

The Dark Parts

Laying on your chest
Tracing the lines
I love the best
Music filling the room
And you move in
To kiss me
Lyrics passing from tongue to tongue
And the words
From the souls of poets
Dancing around us
In the moonlight
A part of me
Can stay here...
The dark parts
Still needing licking
From the wounds

A Black Negligee

Tied hands
Hips that bend
Grab that python
Make it spend
Ice drips
From my lips
Collects in pools
Between sips
Riding high
Queen on her throne
Draining it dry
And bringing him home

The Writer

You picked me up
And placed me between
The paragraphs of your day
You kept my love
Like notes
In the margins of your thoughts
And bookmarked our memories
A nostalgic essay

Little Spoon

All dried up
The words that used
To flow like honey
Sticky with the sweet heat
Of desire
Dripping between
Mounds
Collecting in pools
And ready to eat
And you waiting
With your spoon

Siren

Like rocks
Smoothed by the river
And golden from the sun
Each finger an elegant
Extension of some man's son
Gripping tight
Round her waist
Tracing edges and tasting skin
Rocky ridges and jagged cliffs
Another shipwreck for the siren

The Healer

I
am

Beautiful Adventure

Travel over
The hills and valleys
of my legs
With gentle fingers
Make me cum
Until I beg
Then collapse under the stars
And share a breath
Then rest from the journey
And in my hands, your head

Eclipse

Pouring out into the night
And onto the sand
All that's left between us stands
A question ever evolving
Like the eclipse of the moon
And too soon
Time tiks its final tok
And the questions
Left
Buried in the sand
Under the red and hazy strands
Of the moon's light

Lovers in Technicolor

Blazing across the midnight sky
Stars shine and zoom by
Smiling lines of laughter's past
On a face with 2 sides
2 hearts beating in sync
One breath in
Then another time
And hands entangled
In the moonlight
Telling stories
Between yearning eyes

Delicious

Rolling over
Each letter
Of your name
You leave
A delicious taste
In my mouth
And leave me
Wanting more

Queen of Pentacles

A Queen of Pentacles
On her throne
Tendrils that curl
With comfort
And nurturing tones
Holding fast
To the mast of all that she's known
Her violet crown
Opens and is ready to bestow
Love to all
Who stands before her

Our Love

Our love
Wasn't like a storm
That tears through your heart
It was like a soft summer rain
In the late afternoon
That sets the day into parts
Our love
Was like a blanket
You wrap yourself in at night
Like the pillow
That's waiting for you
To rest your bones
And whispers of atonement
Our love
Wasn't loud and bright
With vibrant colors of laughter
Like a carnival
Of endless and exciting rides
Our love
Was like the predictable
Routines of night
Our love was like the subtle shades
And quiet
Of the moonlight

Poles Apart

That invisible glow
That exudes from your insides
To bask in that light...
And the drips that spill
Out from your fingers and toes
To catch them...
And roll them over on my tongue
Attracted to the gravity
Inside your poles
To dance...
With the essence of your soul

Possibilities

In the way the white blooms fall
Against the cornflower blue
Of a single wall
I love you
Like the possibilities
Of all that is beautiful to behold
And never seen
Possibilities of the many
That are destined to meet
But never destined to be

Death

Grab my neck
With both hands
Crashing into you
Like waves to sand
My lips apart
A fist full of hair
And me drowning
In your stare
Give it to me
All of you
The animal inside
I love too
A heavy collapse
And me on your chest
Following the lines
I love best
Made with hurt
Made with pain
Healing each one
With my trace
Voices carried
By the moon
As the god's listen
A lover's tune

In a Dream

The night we met
And all around the room
Chats and lights and music
But sweeter was the sound
Of our laughter
And later
When we parted
In the quiet still of the night
As the moon rose high
Your voice filled my dreams
With energy and possibilities
Telling me all about the days
That I missed
Telling me all about the days
Before we met

Drive

A name whispered in lights
In shades of red and whites
Along a glistening highway
And through the rain
I'm reminded of you
Wipers sway
And erase away the memories
One after another
A rhythmic succession
Swatting down
Each pitch of thought
But behind the clouds
A piece of sky peeks out
Blue as your eyes
And I am reminded
Even after the storm
Pieces of you
Will be in everything

Enchanting Ghost

Your enchanting ghost
Haunts every thought
And rests heavy
Behind my cage
Breathing in
Breathing out
With each heartbeat
And prickling up from within
The skin I'm covered in

The Empress

Breathing the breath
From the winds
Of each season
The empress moves
Peppered cheeks
And golden rays of summer
On her skin
The rebirthing
Of all the hopes of Spring
Is at her fingertips
And when the falling dreams
Of autumn
One by one
Drift around her golden hair
Winter is where
She makes ready her rest
Within the trees
That are bare
of all the memories
of her life

Am I Pretty?

Am I pretty?
With my worry lines
And harsh stare
Behind honey eyes
Am I sweet?
With my eager mouth
And biting teeth
Making you bleed
Am I soft?
With my rough edges
Whispering heavy words
Bruising your knees
Am I sharp?
Did you cut yourself?
Am I a nuisance
To feed?

Empty Spaces

Your seed
Fills in me
A Need
For you
To love me

Moonflower

Pound away
Into the deep places
That stop my heart
And make the breath catch
At the top of my throat
Like a Cereus
Open and wanting
In the moonlight
My pistol quivers
And awaits
For you

www.ingramcontent.com/pod-product-compliance
Lightning Source LLC
LaVergne TN
LVHW012250070526
838201LV00107B/317/J